Jams, Jellies & Preserves

by Sue Ashworth
Illustrated by Christine Wilson

First published in Great Britain in 1995 by
Parragon Book Service Ltd
Unit 13–17
Avonbridge Trading Estate
Atlantic Road
Avonmouth
Bristol BS11 9QD

ISBN 0-7525-0762-1

Conceived, designed and produced by Haldane Mason, London

Printed in Italy

Note: Cup measurements in this book are for American cups. Tablespoons are assumed to be 15ml.
Unless otherwise stated, milk is assumed to be full-fat and eggs are standard size 2 (AA large).

CONTENTS

CLASSIC STRAWBERRY CONSERVE

MAKES 6 x 500 g/1 lb JARS

2 kg/4 lb/3 quarts fresh strawberries, hulled

2 kg/4 lb/8 cups granulated sugar

Whole fruit is used to make a conserve, and the finished consistency is thinner and more syrupy than that of a jam. This homemade conserve is a real treat – make some to spoon on to warm, fresh scones (biscuits).

1 Place alternate layers of strawberries and sugar in a very large bowl (or use 2 smaller bowls). Cover and leave in a cool place for 24 hours.

2 Transfer the strawberry mixture to a large, heavy-based saucepan. Heat gently, stirring occasionally, until sugar is dissolved. Boil steadily for 5 minutes.

3 Remove from the heat, then return the mixture to the bowl. Cover with a clean, damp tea towel (dishcloth) and leave in a cool place for 2 days.

4 Transfer the mixture to the saucepan once more. Bring to the boil, then boil steadily for 10–20 minutes, until a soft set is reached. To test for a soft set, place a teaspoonful of the conserve on a cold saucer and cool it quickly. Push the surface with your finger – it should crinkle slightly, but should not be at all stiff.

5 Sterilize the jars by washing them in hot, soapy water. Rinse in hot water, then place them in a preheated oven at 120°C/250°F/Gas mark ½ until they are needed.

6 Leave the conserve to stand for 15–20 minutes, then stir to distribute the fruit. Pour into the warmed, sterilized jars, seal and label.

BLACKCURRANT JAM

Blackcurrants are one of the finest fruits for jam making. They have a delicious sharp-sweet flavour, and a high pectin content, which helps the jam to set.

MAKES 6 x 500 g / 1 lb JARS

1 kg/2 lb/2 quarts blackcurrants

900 ml/1½ pints/3½ cups water

1.5 kg/3 lb/6 cups granulated sugar

1 Check over the fruit to remove any stalks and leaves, but avoid washing the fruit unless really necessary. Put into a preserving pan or a very large saucepan with the water. Heat and simmer gently for 30–40 minutes to soften the fruit and release the pectin, which helps the jam to set.

2 Add the sugar to the blackcurrants and let it dissolve, stirring occasionally. Bring to the boil and boil rapidly until setting point is reached – about 15–20 minutes. Skim off any scum, not foam, towards the end of cooking time. To test for setting point, spoon a little jam on to a cold saucer and cool it quickly. Push the jam with your finger – it should crinkle on the surface, but should not be stiff. Double check by putting a drop of cooled jam on the end of your finger. If the jam does not run off, it is ready.

3 When the jam has reached setting point

remove it from the heat and allow it to settle for a few minutes. Stir, then pour into warmed, sterilized jars (see page 4). Seal and label. The jam will set as it cools.

GOOSEBERRY JAM

This is a true country-style jam, which creates delightful memories of hot, hazy midsummer days when you eat it in the middle of winter.

MAKES 10 x 500 g/1 lb JARS

2 kg/4 lb/scant 3 quarts gooseberries, not too ripe

750 ml/1¼ pints/3 cups water

10–12 heads of elderflowers (optional)

3–4 sprigs of tansy (optional)

2.5 kg/5 lb/10 cups granulated sugar

1 Top and tail the gooseberries. Place them in a very large saucepan or preserving pan and add the water. Carefully rinse the elderflower heads and tansy (if using), then tie them in a muslin (cheesecloth) bag. Add to the saucepan. Heat and simmer gently, stirring occasionally, until the fruit is soft and tender – about 20–30 minutes.

2 Meanwhile, place the sugar in a large heatproof bowl. Transfer to a preheated oven 150°C/300°F/Gas mark 2 for 15–20 minutes to warm through.

3 Remove the saucepan from the heat and lift out the muslin (cheesecloth) bag, squeezing out any juice from the bag back into the saucepan. Discard the bag. Add the warmed sugar to the saucepan and leave it to dissolve, stirring gently from time to time.

4 Return the saucepan to the heat and bring to the boil. Boil steadily until setting point is reached. To test for setting point, spoon a little jam onto a cold saucer and cool it quickly. Push the surface of the jam with your finger – it should crinkle, but should not be stiff.

5 Remove the pan from the heat and let the jam settle for a few minutes. Stir to distribute the fruit evenly, then pour into warmed, sterilized jars (see page 4). Seal and label.

RASPBERRY & REDCURRANT JAM

Ripe summer fruits combine perfectly to give a clear, bright jam that makes a beautiful spread for fresh bread, toast and scones (biscuits).

1 Pick over the raspberries and redcurrants, discarding any stalks. Put them into a very large saucepan or preserving pan with the water. Heat gently and simmer until the fruit is softened, about 20–25 minutes. Remove the saucepan from the heat.

2 Add the sugar to the fruit and stir until dissolved. Return the saucepan to the heat and bring the mixture to the boil. Boil rapidly until setting point is reached. To test for setting point, spoon a little jam on to a cold saucer and cool it quickly. Push the surface of the jam with your finger – it should crinkle, but should not be stiff.

3 Remove the pan from the heat and leave the jam to settle for a few minutes. Stir to distribute the fruit evenly, then pour into warmed, sterilized jars (see page 4). Seal and label.

10

Raspberry & Redcurrant Jam

11

SUMMER PUDDING JAM

Make the most of the wonderful variety of soft summer fruit by preserving some in this superb jam. Strawberries, raspberries, blackcurrants and redcurrants are perfect because they taste so good together!

MAKES 6 x 500 g / 1 lb JARS

1 kg/2 lb/2 quarts blackcurrants

500 g/1 lb/1½ pints strawberries, hulled

250 g/8 oz/2 cups redcurrants

250 g/8 oz/2 cups raspberries

1.5 litres/2½ pints/1½ quarts water

3 kg/6 lb/12 cups granulated sugar

1 Remove any stalks and leaves from the fruit, but avoid washing it unless really necessary. Put it into a preserving pan or very large saucepan with the water. Heat and simmer gently for 30–40 minutes. This softens the fruit and releases the pectin, which helps the jam to set.

2 Remove pan from the heat. Add the sugar to the fruit and leave to dissolve completely, stirring the mixture from time to time. Bring to the boil and boil rapidly until setting point is reached – about 15–20 minutes. Skim off any scum towards the end of cooking time. To test for setting point, spoon a little jam on to a cold saucer and cool it quickly. Push the jam with your finger – it should crinkle on the surface, but should not be stiff.

3 Pour the jam into warmed, sterilized jars (see page 4), then seal and label. The jam will set as it cools.

Summer Pudding Jam

13

BLACKBERRY & APPLE JAM

Blackberries growing wild are combined with windfall apples to make this into a very economical, yet extremely delicious recipe for jam.

MAKES 10 x 500 g/1 lb JARS

2 kg/4 lb blackberries

300 ml/½ pint/1¼ cups water

1 kg/2 lb cooking apples

3 kg/6 lb/12 cups granulated sugar

1 Pick over the blackberries, discarding any stalks. Put them into a very large saucepan or preserving pan with half the water. Heat gently and simmer until the fruit is softened, about 20–25 minutes.

2 Meanwhile, peel, core and chop the apples and cook them in a separate saucepan with the remaining water, until soft. Add the apples to the blackberries, stir together, then remove the saucepan from the heat.

3 Add the sugar to the fruit and stir until dissolved. Return the saucepan to the heat and bring the mixture to the boil. Boil rapidly until setting point is reached. To test for setting point, spoon a little jam on to a cold saucer and cool it quickly. Push the surface of the jam with your finger – it should crinkle, but should not be stiff.

4 Remove the pan from the heat and leave the jam to settle for a few minutes. Stir to

distribute the fruit evenly, then
pour into warmed, sterilized jars
(see page 4). Seal and label.

15

AUTUMN FRUIT JAM

In this jam, a combination of autumn fruits is used to make a preserve with an excellent flavour. Choose apples, pears and plums that are not over-ripe for the best flavour and consistency.

MAKES 10 x 500 g/1 lb JARS

1.5 kg/3 lb cooking apples

1 kg/2 lb pears

300 ml/½ pint/1¼ cups water

1 kg/2 lb plums

3 kg/6 lb/12 cups granulated sugar

1 Peel, core and chop the apples and pears, and put them into a very large saucepan or preserving pan with the water. Halve and stone (pit) the plums and add them to the saucepan.

2 Heat gently and simmer until the fruit is softened, about 20–25 minutes. Remove the saucepan from the heat.

3 Add the sugar to the fruit and stir until dissolved. Return the saucepan to the heat and bring to the boil. Boil rapidly until setting point is reached. To test for setting point, spoon a little jam on to a cold saucer and cool it quickly. Push the surface of the jam with your finger – it should crinkle, but should not be stiff.

4 Remove the pan from the heat and leave the jam to settle for a few minutes. Stir to distribute the fruit evenly, then pour into warmed, sterilized jars (see page 4). Seal and label.

RHUBARB & CRAB-APPLE JAM

This delightful jam is made with a combination of rhubarb and crab-apples. Cinnamon and fresh ginger root lend a lovely, subtle fragrance and flavour.

MAKES 10 x 500 g/1 lb JARS

2.5 kg/5 lb rhubarb, trimmed and chopped

300 ml/½ pint/1¼ cups water

1 kg/2 lb crab-apples

1½ tbsp lemon juice

3 kg/6 lb/12 cups granulated sugar

1 tsp ground cinnamon

2 tsp chopped fresh ginger root (or 1 tsp ground ginger)

1 Put the rhubarb into a very large saucepan or preserving pan with the water. Heat gently and simmer until the fruit is softened, about 10–15 minutes.

2 Meanwhile, peel, core and chop the crab-apples. Add them to the saucepan with the lemon juice, stir together, and cook until softened, about 30 minutes. Remove the saucepan from the heat.

3 Add the sugar to the fruit and stir until dissolved. Return the saucepan to the heat and bring the mixture to the boil. Boil rapidly until setting point is reached. To test for setting point, spoon a little jam on to a cold saucer and cool it quickly. Push the surface of the jam with your finger – it should crinkle, but should not be stiff.

4 Remove the pan from the heat and leave the jam to settle for a few minutes. Stir to distribute the fruit evenly, then add the cinnamon and ginger,

stirring well to mix thoroughly.
Pour into warmed, sterilized jars
(see page 4). Seal and label.

DAMSON JAM

Tart-flavoured damsons look like small bluish-purple plums. They make the most marvellous jam, with a dark, rich colour.

MAKES 8 x 500 g/1 lb JARS

2 kg/4 lb damsons

750 ml/1¼ pints/3 cups water

2.5 kg/5 lb/10 cups granulated sugar

1 Put the damsons into a very large saucepan or preserving pan. Do not attempt to remove the stones (pits) at this stage as it is easier to take them out later when the fruit has softened.

2 Add the water and bring to the boil, then reduce the heat and simmer gently until the fruit is soft and the contents of the pan are reduced by one-third. Skim off the stones (pits) as they float to the surface. Remove the saucepan from the heat.

3 Add the sugar and stir until dissolved. Return to the heat and bring to the boil. Boil rapidly until setting point is reached. To test for setting point, spoon a little jam on to a cold saucer and cool it quickly. Push the surface of the jam with your finger – it should crinkle, but should not be stiff.

4 Remove the pan from the heat and leave the jam to settle for a few minutes. Stir to distribute the fruit evenly, then pour into warmed, sterilized jars (see page 4). Seal and label.

20

GREENGAGE PRESERVE

Greengages are small green plums which have a golden hue when fully ripe. If you enjoy plum jam then this recipe could become one of your favourites.

1 Cut the greengages in half and remove their stones (pits). Put the fruit into a very large saucepan or preserving pan. Remove some of the kernels from the stones (pits) and add them to the pan with the water. (The pectin contained in the kernels helps the jam to set.)

2 Heat gently and simmer until the fruit is soft and the contents of the pan are reduced by about one-third. Remove the saucepan from the heat.

3 Add the sugar and stir until dissolved, then return the pan to the heat. Bring to the boil and boil rapidly until setting point is reached. To test for setting point, spoon a little jam on to a cold saucer and cool it quickly. Push the surface of the jam with your finger – it should crinkle, but should not be stiff.

4 Remove the pan from the heat and leave the jam to settle for a few minutes. Stir to distribute the fruit evenly, then pour into warmed, sterilized jars (see page 4). Seal and label.

PLUM JAM

3 kg/6 lb medium red plums

450 ml/¾ pint/scant 2 cups water

3 kg/6 lb/12 cups granulated sugar

Prepare this jam when plums are plentiful. It makes a wonderful topping for sponge (baked) puddings, and tastes divine with fresh homemade scones (biscuits).

1 Cut the plums in half and remove their stones (pits). Put the fruit into a very large saucepan or preserving pan. Remove some of the kernels from the stones (pits) and add them to the pan with the water. (The kernels give the jam a delicious almond flavour and the pectin contained in them helps the jam to set.)

2 Heat gently and simmer until the plums are soft and the contents of the saucepan are reduced by about a third. Remove the pan from the heat.

3 Add the sugar and stir until dissolved, then return the pan to the heat. Bring to the boil and boil rapidly until setting point is reached. To test for setting point, spoon a little jam on to a cold saucer and cool it quickly. Push the surface of the jam with your finger – it should crinkle, but should not be stiff.

4 Remove the pan from the heat and leave the jam to settle for a few minutes. Skim off as many kernels as possible, then stir to distribute

the fruit evenly. Pour into warmed, sterilized jars (see page 4). Seal and label.

APRICOT & BRANDY CONSERVE

This conserve has a splash of apricot brandy added to give it a bit of a kick. It is lovely to have around at Christmas, when you can have some for breakfast with warm croissants and rolls.

1 Chop the apples roughly, without peeling or coring them. Put them into a large, heavy-based saucepan with the water and heat gently. Simmer, stirring occasionally, until the fruit is very soft – about 1 hour.

2 Strain the fruit through a nylon sieve (strainer) and retain the strained juice and pulp. (This makes use of the high pectin content of cooking apples. When the juice and pulp are added to the apricots, the pectin enables the conserve to set.) Discard the peel, pith and pips (seeds).

3 Put the apricots into a large, heavy-based saucepan or preserving pan with the strained apple juice and pulp. Heat and simmer gently until the fruit is very soft, about 30–40 minutes. Remove from the heat.

4 Add the sugar and stir until dissolved. Return the saucepan to the heat and bring to the boil. Boil rapidly until a soft set is reached. To test for this, spoon a little conserve on to a cold saucer and cool it quickly. Push the surface with your finger – it should crinkle slightly, but should not be at all stiff.

5 Remove the pan from the heat and leave to settle for a few minutes. Stir in the apricot brandy, then pour the conserve into warmed, sterilized jars (see page 4). Seal and label.

PEACH & HAZELNUT PRESERVE

MAKES 7 x 500 g/1 lb JARS

1 kg/2 lb cooking apples

600 ml/1 pint/2½ cups water

2 kg/4 lb fresh peaches

2 kg/4 lb/8 cups granulated sugar

125 g/4 oz/1 cup hazelnuts, halved

Fresh peaches make beautiful jam that tastes very special. This version has a few halved hazelnuts in it, which add an element of luxury to the finished jam.

1 Chop the apples, without peeling or coring them. Put them into a large, heavy-based saucepan with the water and heat gently. Simmer, stirring occasionally, until the fruit is very soft – about 30 minutes.

2 Strain the fruit through a nylon sieve (strainer) and retain the strained juice and pulp. (This procedure makes use of the high pectin content of cooking apples. When the juice and pulp are added to the peaches, the pectin helps the preserve to set.) Discard the peel, pith and pips (seeds).

3 Cut the peaches and into quarters, removing their stones (pits). Put the peaches into a large, heavy-based saucepan or preserving pan with the apple juice and pulp. Heat and simmer gently for about 20 minutes to soften the peaches, stirring occasionally. Remove the saucepan from the heat.

4 Add the sugar to the pan and stir until dissolved. Add the hazelnuts, then return to the heat and bring to the boil. Boil rapidly until setting point is reached (see page 6).

5 Remove the pan from the heat and leave the jam to

settle for about 15 minutes. Stir to distribute the fruit and nuts evenly, then pour into warmed, sterilized jars (see page 4). Seal and label.

KUMQUAT & PASSION FRUIT PRESERVE

Kumquats look like tiny oval oranges. They have a very thin skin and can be eaten whole, although they are quite tart. In this delicious recipe they are married with the flavour of passion fruit to create an exotic jam.

1 Slice the kumquats in half. Put them into a large, heavy-based saucepan with the water. Heat and simmer gently for about 1 hour, until the fruit is very soft. Remove the saucepan from the heat.

2 Add the lemon juice and sugar to the saucepan and stir until the sugar has dissolved. Return the saucepan to the heat and bring the mixture to the boil. Boil rapidly until setting point is reached. To test for setting point, spoon a little jam on to a cold saucer and cool it quickly. Push the surface of the jam with your finger – it should crinkle, but should not be stiff.

3 Remove the pan from the heat and leave the jam to settle for a few minutes. Add the pulp and seeds from the passion fruit and stir to distribute the fruit evenly. Pour into small, warmed, sterilized jars (see page 4). Seal and label.

PEAR & GINGER JAM

Stem (candied) ginger in syrup gives a delicious flavour to this unusual pear jam. Choose firm pears in preference to ones that are very ripe.

MAKES 10 x 500 g/1 lb JARS

2 kg/4 lb firm pears

750 g/1½ lb baking apples

finely grated rind of 1 lemon

4 tbsp lemon juice

1.25 litres/2¼ pints/5 cups water

3 kg/6 lb/12 cups granulated sugar

90 g/3 oz/¾ cup stem (candied) ginger in syrup, drained and chopped finely

1 Peel and core the pears and apples, retaining both the peel and the cores. Tie the peel and cores in a muslin (cheesecloth) bag. Chop the fruit roughly.

2 Put the fruit into a very large saucepan or preserving pan with the lemon rind and juice. Add the water and the muslin (cheesecloth) bag. Bring to the boil, then reduce the heat and simmer gently until the fruit is tender, about 30 minutes.

3 Remove the saucepan from the heat and lift out the muslin (cheesecloth) bag, squeezing any juice from it back into the pan. Discard the bag. Add the sugar to the saucepan and stir gently until dissolved.

4 Return the pan to the heat and bring to the boil. Boil rapidly until setting point is reached. To test for setting point, spoon a little jam on to a cold saucer and cool it quickly. Push the jam with your finger – it should crinkle on the surface, but should not be stiff.

5 Leave the jam to settle for 15 minutes, then add the ginger. Stir to distribute the fruit

and ginger. Pour into warmed, sterilized jars (see page 4). Seal and label.

FIG & WALNUT CONSERVE

This delightful Fig & Walnut Conserve tastes excellent with toast or fresh rolls at breakfast time. Try a little spooned on to creamy rice pudding or semolina to make a delicious dessert.

MAKES 4 x 500 g/1 lb JARS

1 kg/2 lb fresh figs, quartered

finely grated rind of 2 lemons

75 ml/3 fl oz/⅓ cup lemon juice

4 tbsp water

1 kg/2 lb/4 cups granulated sugar

60 g/2 oz/½ cup walnut halves

1 Put the figs into a large heavy-based saucepan with the lemon rind and juice. Add the water and cook over a gentle heat, stirring occasionally, until the figs are soft.

2 Meanwhile, place the sugar in a large heatproof bowl. Place in a preheated oven at 150°C/300°F/Gas mark 2 for 15–20 minutes to warm through.

3 Tip the warmed sugar into the figs and stir gently to avoid breaking up the fruit. Heat until the sugar has dissolved, then bring to the boil. Boil the mixture steadily until a soft set is reached. To test for a soft set, place a teaspoonful of the conserve on to a cold saucer and cool it quickly. Push the surface with your finger – it should crinkle slightly, but should not be at all stiff.

4 Leave the conserve for 10–15 minutes to let it settle, then add the walnuts. Stir gently to distribute the fruit and nuts, then pour into warmed, sterilized jars (see page 4). Seal and label.

Fig & Walnut Conserve

PINEAPPLE JAM

This jam uses canned crushed pineapple for speed, convenience and economy. It has a great flavour and tastes good in sandwiches, especially with some sliced banana. You can also use this jam for cake fillings or for spreading on toast.

MAKES 3 x 500 g/1 lb JARS

2 kg/4 lb/8 cups canned crushed pineapple in natural juice

4 tbsp lemon juice

2 kg/4 lb/8 cups granulated sugar

1 Put the pineapple and lemon juice into a large, heavy-based saucepan. Heat and simmer gently, uncovered, until thickened and pulpy. Remove the saucepan from the heat.

2 Add the sugar and stir until dissolved. Return the saucepan to the heat and bring to the boil. Boil rapidly until setting point is reached. To test for setting point, spoon a little jam on to a cold saucer and cool it quickly. Push the surface of the jam with your finger – it should crinkle, but should not be stiff.

3 Leave the jam to settle for a few minutes, then stir. Pour into warmed, sterilized jars (see page 4). Seal and label.

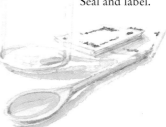

SEVILLE ORANGE MARMALADE

At the end of the winter, fill the house with the wonderful, bitter-sweet aroma of Seville oranges as they cook to make this most delicious marmalade.

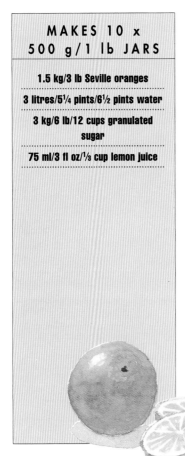

MAKES 10 x 500 g / 1 lb JARS

1.5 kg/3 lb Seville oranges

3 litres/5¼ pints/6½ pints water

3 kg/6 lb/12 cups granulated sugar

75 ml/3 fl oz/⅓ cup lemon juice

1 Cut the oranges in half and squeeze the juice. Place the pips (seeds) in a muslin (cheesecloth) bag and tie securely. Shred the peel thinly, without removing the pith. Put the peel, juice, muslin (cheesecloth) bag and water into a very large saucepan or preserving pan.

2 Heat and simmer gently for about 2 hours, until the peel is very tender and the contents of the pan are reduced by about one-third. Remove the saucepan from the heat.

3 Lift the muslin (cheesecloth) bag from the pan and squeeze it to extract the juice, then discard the bag. Add the sugar and lemon juice to the saucepan and stir until the sugar has dissolved, then return the pan to the heat. Bring to the boil, then boil rapidly until setting point is reached. To test for setting point, spoon a little marmalade on to a cold saucer and cool it quickly. Push the surface of the marmalade with your finger – it should crinkle, but should not be stiff.

4 Skim off any scum from the surface of the marmalade, then remove the pan from the

heat. Leave the marmalade to settle for about 15 minutes, then stir to distribute the shreds evenly. Pour into warmed, sterilized jars (see page 4). Seal and label.

SHARP CITRUS MARMALADE

Grapefruit, oranges and limes make this sharp, tangy marmalade. Shred the peel very finely to make it look attractive in the finished preserve.

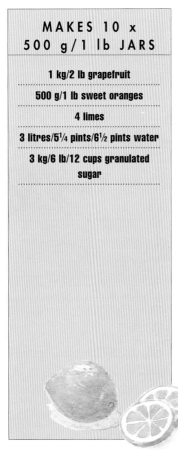

MAKES 10 x 500 g / 1 lb JARS

1 kg/2 lb grapefruit

500 g/1 lb sweet oranges

4 limes

3 litres/5¼ pints/6½ pints water

3 kg/6 lb/12 cups granulated sugar

1 Peel the grapefruit and oranges, then cut the pith away from the peel. Halve the limes and squeeze the juice. Finely shred the peel from all the fruit and put into a large saucepan or preserving pan with the lime juice and half the water. Heat and simmer gently until the peel is very tender, about 2 hours.

2 Chop the flesh and pith from the grapefruit and oranges and place in a large saucepan with the remaining water. Heat and simmer gently, covered, for about 1¼ hours. Strain through a nylon sieve (strainer) or colander, then add the strained mixture to the shreds in the other saucepan (after they have cooked for 2 hours). Remove the pan from the heat.

3 Add the sugar to the pan and stir until dissolved. Return the pan to the heat and bring to the boil. Boil rapidly until setting point is reached (see page 6).

4 Skim off any scum from the surface of the marmalade, then remove the pan from the heat. Leave the marmalade to settle for about 15 minutes, then

stir to distribute the shreds evenly. Pour into warmed, sterilized jars (see page 4). Seal and label.

WHISKY MAC MARMALADE

This is strictly a marmalade for the grown-ups, with its sophisticated flavours of bitter Seville oranges, stem (candied) ginger, Scotch whisky and ginger wine.

MAKES 10 x 500 g/1 lb JARS

1.5 kg/3 lb Seville oranges

2.5 litres/4¼ pints/2½ quarts water

3 kg/6 lb/12 cups granulated sugar

4 tbsp lemon juice

60 g/2 oz/½ cup stem (candied) ginger in syrup, drained and chopped

60 ml/2 fl oz/¼ cup ginger wine

120 ml/4 fl oz/½ cup Scotch whisky

1 Cut the oranges in half and squeeze the juice. Place the pips (seeds) into a muslin (cheesecloth) bag and tie securely. Shred the peel thinly, without removing the pith. Put the peel, juice, bag and water into a very large, heavy-based saucepan or preserving pan.

2 Heat and simmer gently for about 2 hours, until the peel is very tender and the contents of the pan are reduced by about one-third. Remove the saucepan from the heat.

3 Lift the muslin (cheesecloth) bag from the pan and squeeze it to extract the juice, then discard the bag. Add the sugar and lemon juice to the saucepan and stir until the sugar has dissolved, then return the pan to the heat. Bring to the boil, then boil rapidly until setting point is reached. To test for setting point, spoon a little marmalade on to a cold saucer and cool it quickly. Push the surface of the marmalade with your finger – it should crinkle, but should not be stiff.

4 Skim off any scum from the surface of the marmalade, then remove the pan from the heat. Leave the marmalade to settle for about 15 minutes, then add the ginger, ginger wine and whisky, stirring well. Pour into warmed, sterilized jars (see page 4). Seal and label.

ORANGE & GRAPEFRUIT CURD

Fresh homemade Orange and Grapefruit Curd is a real treat, especially when spread generously on to crusty new bread or toast for breakfast, or used as a delicious filling for sponge (layer) cakes for afternoon tea.

MAKES 2 x 350 g/12 oz JARS

4 eggs

250 g/8 oz/1 cup caster (superfine) sugar

finely grated rind and juice of 1 large orange

juice of 1 large grapefruit

250 g/8 oz/1 cup unsalted butter, melted

1 In a large heatproof mixing bowl whisk together the eggs, sugar, orange rind and juice and grapefruit juice. Add the warm melted butter and stir together.

2 Set the bowl over a large pan of gently simmering water and stir the mixture with a wooden spoon until it thickens, about 10–15 minutes. Check that it is thick enough by lifting the wooden spoon a little and drizzling the mixture over the surface – it should be thick enough to leave a trail. The curd will thicken more as it cools.

3 Pour into warmed, sterilized jars (see page 4). Seal and label. When completely cool, store in the refrigerator. Use within 4–6 weeks.

Orange & Grapefruit Curd

LEMON & LIME CURD

With its simple ingredients of butter, sugar, eggs and citrus fruit, you couldn't wish for a more delicious spread for fresh bread and scones (biscuits). This recipe is very similar to lemon curd, and includes limes to give a slightly sharper flavour.

MAKES 2 x 350 g / 12 oz JARS

4 eggs

250 g/8 oz/1 cup caster (superfine) sugar

finely grated rind of 2 large lemons

75 ml/3 fl oz/⅓ cup lemon juice

finely grated rind of 2 limes

60 ml/2 fl oz/¼ cup lime juice

250 g/8 oz/1 cup unsalted butter

1 Beat the eggs in a large heatproof bowl. Add the caster (superfine) sugar, lemon rind and juice, and lime rind and juice. Cut the butter into pieces and add to the bowl.

2 Set the bowl over a pan of gently simmering water and stir with a wooden spoon until the butter melts and the mixture thickens, about 15–20 minutes. Check that it is thick enough by lifting the wooden spoon a little and drizzling the mixture over the surface – it should be thick enough to leave a trail. The lemon and lime curd will thicken more as it cools.

3 Pour into warmed, sterilized jars (see page 4). Seal and label. When completely cool, store in the refrigerator. Use within 4–6 weeks.

Lemon & Lime Curd

47

BANANA & NECTARINE CURD

Bananas and nectarines give a new slant to an old favourite. If you love lemon curd, then you will enjoy this scrumptious alternative. Children will like this too, spread thickly on slices of fresh bread.

MAKES 2 x 500 g/1 lb JARS

3 large bananas, peeled and chopped

3 nectarines or peaches, peeled, stoned (pitted) and chopped

finely grated rind of 1 lemon

4 tbsp lemon juice

125 g/4 oz/½ cup butter

250 g/8 oz/1 cup caster (superfine) sugar

4 eggs

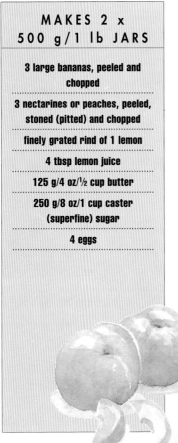

1 Put the bananas and nectarines or peaches into a large saucepan with the lemon rind and juice. Heat gently, stirring often, until the fruit is soft and pulpy – about 5 minutes.

2 Add the butter and sugar to the saucepan and heat gently, stirring, to melt the butter and dissolve the sugar. Transfer the mixture to a large heatproof bowl and leave to cool for 10 minutes.

3 Beat the eggs and stir them into the fruit mixture. Set the bowl over a large saucepan of gently simmering water and cook, stirring with a wooden spoon, until the mixture thickens – about 15–20 minutes. To check that it is thick enough, lift the wooden spoon a little and drizzle the mixture over the surface – it should be thick enough to leave a trail. The banana and nectarine curd will thicken more as it cools.

4 Pour into warmed, sterilized jars (see page 4). Seal and label. When completely cool, store in the refrigerator. Use within 4–6 weeks.

Banana & Nectarine Curd

APPLE BUTTER

MAKES 2 x 500 g/1 lb JARS

1.5 kg/3 lb cooking apples

600 ml/1 pint/2½ cups unsweetened apple juice

about 1 kg/2 lb/4 cups granulated sugar

1 tsp ground mixed (apple pie) spice (optional)

With its soft consistency, Apple Butter makes a delicious spread for fresh bread and scones (biscuits). Once a jar is opened, store it in the refrigerator.

1 Chop the apples roughly, without peeling or coring them. Put them into a large saucepan with the apple juice. Heat and simmer gently, uncovered, until the apples are very soft and pulpy, stirring from time to time. Remove the pan from the heat.

2 Rub the apple pulp through a nylon sieve (strainer), to remove the peel and pips (seeds). Discard what is left in the sieve (strainer) and measure the apple pulp. For each 500 ml/16 fl oz/2 cups apple pulp, measure 350 g/ 12 oz/1½ cups sugar.

3 Return the apple pulp to the saucepan. Heat and simmer until thick, stirring often. Add the sugar and stir until dissolved. Cook gently for 25–35 minutes until there is no liquid left in the pan and a wooden spoon drawn through the middle of the mixture leaves a clear trail. Stir in the mixed (apple pie) spice, if using.

4 Pour into warmed, sterilized jars (see page 4). Top with a waxed disc and seal at once. Label and use within 4 weeks. Once opened, eat within a few days.

SPICED MANGO BUTTER

Treat yourself to some of this smooth Spiced Mango Butter. It tastes superb as an exotic topping for pancakes and waffles with a drizzle of maple syrup, or just try it spread generously on to crusty new bread.

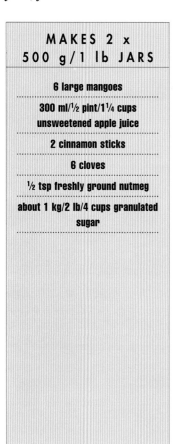

MAKES 2 x 500 g/1 lb JARS

6 large mangoes

300 ml/½ pint/1¼ cups unsweetened apple juice

2 cinnamon sticks

6 cloves

½ tsp freshly ground nutmeg

about 1 kg/2 lb/4 cups granulated sugar

1 Slice the mangoes on each side of their large, flat stones (pits). Chop the flesh roughly, without peeling. Put the fruit into a large saucepan with their stones (pits) and the apple juice. Heat and simmer gently, uncovered, until the mangoes are very soft and pulpy, stirring from time to time. Remove the pan from the heat.

2 Remove the stones (pits) from the saucepan and discard them. Rub the mango pulp through a nylon sieve (strainer), to remove the peel. Discard the contents of the sieve (strainer), and measure the pulp. For each 500 ml/16 fl oz/2 cups mango pulp, measure 350 g/12 oz/1½ cups sugar.

3 Return the mango pulp to the saucepan. Add the cinnamon sticks, cloves and nutmeg. Heat and simmer until thick, stirring often. Add the sugar and stir until dissolved. Cook gently until there is no liquid left in the pan and a wooden spoon drawn through the middle of the mixture leaves a clear trail.

4 Remove the cinnamon sticks from the mixture, then pour

the mango butter into warmed, sterilized jars (see page 4). Top with a waxed disc and seal at once. Label when cool. After opening, store in the refrigerator and use within 3 weeks.

PLUMS IN WINE SYRUP

Choose three different varieties of plum to enhance the appearance of this delicious preserve.

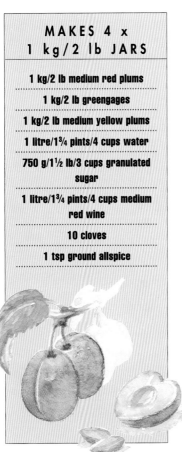

MAKES 4 x 1 kg/2 lb JARS

1 kg/2 lb medium red plums

1 kg/2 lb greengages

1 kg/2 lb medium yellow plums

1 litre/1¾ pints/4 cups water

750 g/1½ lb/3 cups granulated sugar

1 litre/1¾ pints/4 cups medium red wine

10 cloves

1 tsp ground allspice

1 Halve the plums and remove their stones (pits). Pack an equal quantity of each type of plum tightly into sterilized preserving jars.

2 Put the water and sugar into a large saucepan and heat gently, stirring occasionally, until the sugar has dissolved. Bring to the boil and boil for 1 minute. Add the wine and spices, bring back to the boil, then remove from the heat.

3 Pour the wine syrup into the jars to cover the fruit, leaving 1 cm/½ inch space at the top. Tap the jars lightly to let any air bubbles escape. Put the rubber rings and tops on the jars, but not the clips or screw bands.

4 Stand the jars on a baking sheet, leaving plenty of room around each jar for air to circulate. Place in a preheated oven at 150°C/300°F/Gas mark 2 for 50 minutes. Remove the jars from the oven one at a time, putting on the clips or tightening the screw bands at once.

5 To check that a vacuum has been made, leave the jars to stand undisturbed for 24 hours, then remove the clip tops or screw bands. Using the fingers of one hand, pick up the jars by the lid – if the lid comes away a vacuum has not been created. If this happens, the fruit must be eaten straight away, or be processed for a second time.

TRADITIONAL MINCEMEAT

This excellent homemade mincemeat really packs a punch with its rum-soaked fruit! Try some in your mince pies to give them a wonderful flavour.

MAKES 4 x 500 g/1 lb JARS

125 g/4 oz/½ cup glacé (candied) cherries

60 g/2 oz/⅓ cup candied peel

500 g/1 lb/3 cups raisins

350 g/12 oz/2 cups sultanas (golden raisins)

250 g/8 oz/1⅓ cups currants

150 ml/¼ pint/⅔ cup dark rum, brandy or sherry

2 medium dessert (eating) apples

2 tsp mixed (apple pie) spice

½ tsp freshly grated nutmeg

125 g/4 oz/1 cup chopped almonds

250 g/8 oz/1⅓ cups molasses sugar, dark muscovado sugar, or dark brown sugar

250 g/8 oz/1½ cups shredded suet or vegetarian suet

1 Halve the glacé (candied) cherries and chop the candied peel.

2 Put the raisins, sultanas (golden raisins), currants, cherries, candied peel and rum, brandy or sherry into a large bowl, mixing well. Cover and leave in a cool, dark place, stirring occasionally, for 1–2 days.

3 Peel, core and finely chop the apples. Blanch in boiling water for 2 minutes, and then drain well. Add to the soaked dried fruit mixture with the mixed (apple pie) spice, nutmeg and chopped almonds, stirring well.

4 Add the molasses sugar, dark muscovado sugar or dark brown sugar to the fruit mixture and stir well to combine thoroughly. Mix in the suet.

5 Pack into sterilized jars (see page 4). Seal and label.

APPLE & MINT JELLY

Perfect with roast lamb and new potatoes, this jelly also tastes very pleasant with fish and chicken dishes.

MAKES 5 x 500 g / 1 lb JARS

3 kg/6 lb cooking apples

120 ml/4 fl oz/½ cup lemon juice

water

granulated sugar

2 tbsp chopped fresh mint

1 Chop the apples roughly, without peeling or coring them. Put them into a very large saucepan or preserving pan and add the lemon juice. Add just enough cold water to barely cover the apples. Put over a low heat and simmer until the apples are very soft and pulpy – about 1 hour. Remove from the heat.

2 Mash the apples, then pour the mixture into a scalded jelly bag. Leave the mixture to drip through the jelly bag for about 1½ hours, until there are hardly any drips. Do not squeeze the bag.

3 Discard the pulp in the jelly bag. Measure the strained apples, then pour them into the cleaned saucepan or preserving pan and bring to the boil. Remove from the heat.

4 For each 600 ml/1 pint/2½ cups of strained apple, add 500 g/1 lb/2 cups sugar to the saucepan and stir until dissolved. Return to the heat, bring to the boil and boil rapidly until setting point is reached. The mixture should reach 105°C/220°F – test with a sugar (jelly) thermometer. Remove from the heat and leave the mixture to settle for about 15 minutes.

5 Stir in the chopped mint, then pour the jelly into warmed, sterilized jars (see page 4). Seal and label.

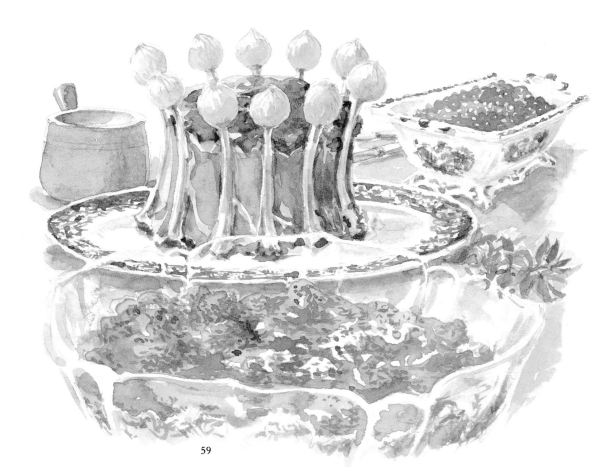

REDCURRANT & ROSEMARY JELLY

Make this superb jelly when redcurrants are plentiful in the summer. The jelly makes an excellent accompaniment to roast pork and cold cooked meats.

1 Put the redcurrants into a large saucepan or preserving pan with the water and lemon juice. Heat gently and simmer until the fruit is very tender, about 30 minutes.

2 Mash the fruit, then pour it into a scalded jelly bag. Leave the mixture to drip through the bag for about 40 minutes, until there are hardly any drips. Do not squeeze.

3 Return the pulp in the jelly bag to the saucepan with a further 300 ml/½ pint/1¼ cups water and simmer for 30 minutes more, then strain the mixture again. Discard the remaining pulp.

4 Mix together the 2 quantities of strained juice, and measure. Pour into the cleaned saucepan or preserving pan and bring to the boil. Remove from the heat. For each 600 ml/1 pint/2½ cups of fruit juice, add 500 g/1 lb/2 cups sugar to the saucepan and stir until dissolved. Return the saucepan to the heat, bring to the boil and boil rapidly until setting point is reached.

The mixture should reach 105°C/ 220°F – test with a sugar (jelly) thermometer.

5 Scald the sprigs of rosemary with boiling water and add a couple of sprigs to each warmed, sterilized jar (see page 4). Pour in the redcurrant jelly. Seal and label.

TAYBERRY VINEGAR

Tayberries look like slightly elongated raspberries, and they are little darker in colour. They make this superb fruit vinegar, which tastes marvellous in salad dressings.

MAKES 1.5 LITRES/3 PINTS

2 kg/4 lb/3 quarts tayberries (or raspberries)

1.25 litres/2¼ pints/5 cups distilled white malt vinegar

about 750 g/1½ lb/3 cups granulated sugar

whole tayberries to decorate (optional)

1 Put the tayberries into a large glass mixing bowl and mash them with a wooden spoon or potato masher. Add the vinegar and stir well. Cover the bowl with clingfilm (plastic wrap) and leave to stand in a cool place for 1 week, stirring several times each day.

2 Strain the mixture through a jelly bag (available from good cook shops). When the bag has stopped dripping, squeeze it to extract as much of the fruit vinegar as possible.

3 Measure the amount of liquid and pour it into a large saucepan. Add 250 g/8 oz/1 cup of sugar to each 600 ml/1 pint/2½ cups of liquid. Heat gently, stirring, to dissolve the sugar, then boil rapidly for 10 minutes.

4 Pour into warmed, sterilized bottles (see page 4). Add a few whole tayberries to each bottle, and seal with vinegar-proof tops.

Tayberry Vinegar

INDEX